Christmas
IDEALS

ideals

NASHVILLE, TENNESSEE

ISBN 0-8249-5866-7

Published by Ideals Publications
A division of Guideposts
535 Metroplex Drive, Suite 250
Nashville, Tennessee 37211
www.idealsbooks.com

Printed and bound in Mexico by RR Donnelley

Editor, Marjorie L. Lloyd
Designer, Marisa Calvin

Cover photo copyright © Steve Terrill

10 9 8 7 6 5 4 3 2 1

ACKNOWLEDGMENTS
BENNETT, DEBORAH, A. "Reverie" from *Mature Years*, Winter 2001. Submitted for use in
Ideals by the author. JAQUES, EDNA. "Snowstorm" from *Roses in December*. Published by
Thomas Allen Ltd., 1952. Used by permission of Louise Bonnell. TROTT, ROSEMARY
CLIFFORD. "To a New House At Christmas," Previously published in *Good Housekeeping*.
Submitted for use in *Ideals* by the author. Our sincere thanks to those authors, or their heirs,
some of whom we were unable to locate, who submitted poems or articles to *Ideals* for publi-
cation. Every possible effort has been made to acknowledge ownership of material used.

$\mathcal{T}$o

_____

$\mathcal{F}$ROM

_____

$\mathcal{D}$ATE

_____

Photograph by Steve Terrill

Wonderful Wintertime
Nora M. Bozeman

Beneath a sky of cobalt blue,
The day is wrapped in winter's hue.
Diamond-sparkled snowflakes fly,
Like frost-kissed magic from on high.

Vivid blue jays, brave and bold,
Hop around and loudly scold.

Cardinals decorate the scene,
On snowy boughs of evergreen.

Icy winds sculpt drifts of white
And etch each silver-frosted night.
December hangs her frozen head
And sleeps upon an ermine bed.

The Lacemaker
Del Turner

In the middle of the night, she came
To weave a pattern on my window pane.
With delicate strands of crystal thread,
She looped and stitched; we slept in bed.
With swirls and scallops, she adorned each space
In the finest beauty of winter lace.

My Son's First Snow

Harry E. Ezell

Pressed against the windowpane,
My baby watches his first snow
With eyes and mouth in wonder wide
At sight of this strange countryside,
All white beneath the sparkling tide
Of freshly falling snow.

Ah, Son, the storms of life with pain
May scar your face and heart, I know;
But may they never from your eyes
Remove the light that in them lies,
As now, in wondering surprise,
You watch the falling snow.

Winters Past

Mary Catherine Johnson

I remember long, long icicles that glittered in the sun,
Like crystals flashing from the eaves of houses, every one!
First stretching longer, day by day,
Then dripping, shrinking, the array
Of sparkling spears a-dangle disappeared, and there were none.

I remember frosty forest ferns upon the window glass,
Those early morning etchings as of jungle leaf and grass,
Which wavered with alarm
And vanished as the air grew warm,
But overnight appeared again with glorious foliage mass.

I remember tall brick chimneys on rooftops everywhere,
And noses pinched by acrid smell of coal smoke in the air,
And watching grimy soot-fall fly
Onto the laundry hung to dry—
And laughing, sliding on the snow as grownups turned to stare.

No TWO MOMENTS ARE
ANY MORE ALIKE THAN
TWO SNOWFLAKES.

—ZORA NEALE HURSTON

Photograph by Carr Clifton

SNOWSTORM

Edna Jaques

The cars go by on softly muted wheels;
    The houses have a homemade country look;
The Church of the Redeemer, there on Bloor,
    Looks like a picture from an ancient book.
The roofs are thatches, with furry layers of snow
    Tacked on like batting at a Christmas show.

White-haloed lampposts stand like sentinels
    Before the sleeping castle of their lord;
A million wires furred with downy white
    Glisten and sparkle like a Christmas cord.
The whole town has a happy, festive air,
    Gay as the dancing at a country fair.

A little boy pulls a scarlet sleigh,
    A lady picks out her way to church,
A bird half-hidden in the shrubbery
    Finds his balance on a snowy perch;
The house across the street changed in the night
    Into a fairy palace—shining, white.

Just for a day, let us be young again,
    And let this gentle peace be truly ours:
The snowy paths, the little gates ajar,
    The quaint, top-heavy look of laden towers,
A city wrapped in cellophane and wool—
    God's Christmas package, strangely beautiful.

Country Winter Fun

Ralph W. Seager

There's a big difference between a country winter and a city one. Out there, winter makes the country over; in the city it is winter that is made over. For young ones, the country winter is wonderful. The white clouds, which formed such fantastic scenes in the summer skies, have come down to earth for the sake of small children. As the sky comes drifting in under our feet, we become unbound from ers they may have later. Frost, ferny and crystalline, presses its face to the window, watching us at our snug play in the evening. It is a confirmation of the belief that we can know life in this separation from our ordinary footmarks; that walking upon the water can be an act of truth as well as a symbolic one; that where no flower is possible, there will be flowers. This is winter in the country.

There is no other time of the year when the sky comes between us and the earth.

---

earth, climbing heavenward on snow-fashioned staircases to go sailing on this whiteness as cousins to the wind. We are the chief participants in weather's detached and fanciful riot of fun. There is no other time of the year when the sky comes between us and the earth. It stays while we walk upon it.

Winter is the white phenomenon. Not only do clouds come down as cushions under our feet, but the very waters stand still and let us walk upon them. Trees that are unleafed and stark against the alabaster scene suddenly flower with crystal blossoms, more elegant, more scintillating than any oth-

It was a good thing that we had barrels in those days instead of the modern steel drums. How else could we have gone sailing down the hardened slopes of winter? Solid oak staves were our need, and how my sister and I begged for Dad to declare one of the barrels in the barn as ours. It is not the easiest work in the world to persuade a staunch barrel to give up its shape, to let loose of its hoops and wire, to collapse in a heap. But we had the resources of desire on our side. We must fly on the great clouds.

The outside bend of the stave was worked over with sandpaper, scraped with pieces of broken glass until hand-smooth, then rubbed thoroughly with paraffin. Next, a toe strap was nailed across the width of the stave. Fastening that toe strap was the critical point of the entire operation. Putting a nail into the narrowness of that hard core oak without splitting it required patience, persistence, and a small thumb.

Our winter footwear consisted of high, four-buckle arctics. With these we wore long, black leggings. There must have been a dozen buttons on either side of these leggings, and the buttonholes were always wearing too big. By the time the top button was in its place, the first one had popped out. Sweaters, coats, and mufflers smothered us nose-deep. Our mittens were tethered to each other by a string that ran up one sleeve, around the neck, and back down through the other sleeve. Stocking caps were pulled down over ears. It was impossible to fall down and get hurt. The problem really was, could you get up again?

The staves were heavy, cumbersome, and curved like a chair rocker. It was like riding downhill with a rocking horse under each foot. Off we would go, my sister and I, with these awkward wings on our feet.

Image provided by Fine Art Photographic Library, Ltd., London

At the top of the drift we looked down across the icy polish of the field, turned our stave-skis in a straight-ahead direction, and shoved off. It was a teetering, tongue-biting ride. We were seldom perpendicular. A successful descent was a triumph.

Then back up for another try.

Barrel staves, oaken wings, red-cheeked cherubim sliding on frozen clouds, fire in our faces, chilblain on our toes, laughter, and love—everything was there in my country winter.

BITS & PIECES

I have forgotten much,
but still remember
The poinsettia's red . . .
— *Claude McKay*

Winter comes to rule the varied year.
— *James Thomson*

The splendor of silence—of snow-jeweled hills and of ice.
— *Ingram Crockett*

It is the sea that whitens the roof.
The sea drifts through the winter air.
It is the sea that the north wind makes.
The sea is in the falling snow.
— *Wallace Stevens*

Snow, snow over the whole
land across all boundaries.
— *Boris Pasternak*

Round and round,
like a dance of snow
In a dazzling drift . . .
— *Robert Browning*

At Christmas I no more desire a rose
Than wish a snow in May's newfangled shows,
But like of each thing that in season grows.
— *William Shakespeare*

Christmas is here:
Winds whistle shrill,
Icy and chill.
Little care we;
Little we fear
Weather without,
Shelter'd about
The Mahogany Tree.
— *William Makepeace Thackeray*

I'm dreaming of a white Christmas,
Just like the ones I used to know. . . .
— *Irving Berlin*

And when a snowflake finds a tree,
"Good-day!" it says,"Good-day to thee!
Thou art so bare and lonely, dear,
I'll rest and call my comrades here."
— *Mary Mapes Dodge*

Christmas Valley

Elizabeth Swain Lawson

I stand on a hill, looking downward
To the snowy valley below;
I see smoke spirals from chimneys
And windows with candles' warm glow.

Children skate on a shallow pond,
Within the churchyard's domain,
And men ride upon wood-piled sleds
With Old Dobbin pulling the reins.

As I scan the slope nearest me,
Youths are merrily bobsledding,
And little creatures of the wood
Deep in their nests are bedding.

And I feel a sweet awareness
Of a Presence from above,
Whose birth in lowly Bethlehem
Filled all the world with love.

I pick up my little fir tree
Because twilight is drawing near
And wend home down a snowy path
For the happiest time of year.

Photograph by William H. Johnson

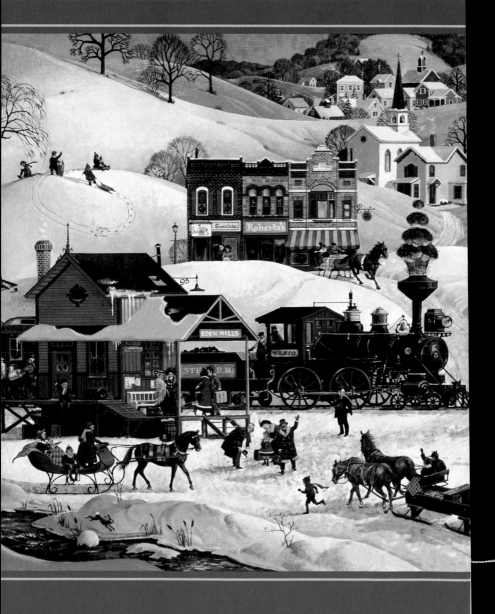

Simple Joys

Sandi Keaton-Wilson

A cedar bough,
A candle lit,
A rocking chair
In which to sit,

A glowing hearth,
A loving smile,
Companionship
To pass the while,

An open book,
A kitten's purr,
Simmering pot
To sniff and stir,

A baby's laugh,
A grandma's tale,

A dust of snow
On front-porch rail,

A whispered prayer,
A whistled carol,
A biting wind
And warm apparel,

A childhood game,
A lifelong friend,
A cheerful card
To sign and send—

These simple joys
Are much the reason
For celebrating
The Christmas season.

Coming Home

Lois J. Martinec

The fine-line script of chimney smoke
Writes "Welcome" in the sky.
This country road brings memories
As miles go skimming by.
There are thoughts of gentle living,
Of scenes from Christmas past,
Of sounds so warm and homey,
Where roots hold deep and fast.
What bonds of love bind and keep,
Time and distance cannot separate.
I'm coming home; it's Christmas,
Where loved ones live and wait.

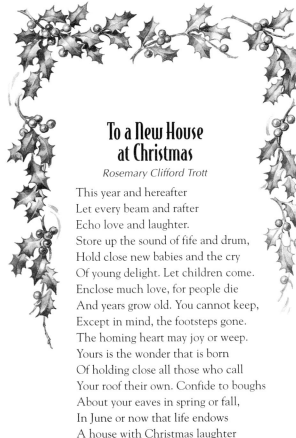

To a New House at Christmas

Rosemary Clifford Trott

This year and hereafter
Let every beam and rafter
Echo love and laughter.
Store up the sound of fife and drum,
Hold close new babies and the cry
Of young delight. Let children come.
Enclose much love, for people die
And years grow old. You cannot keep,
Except in mind, the footsteps gone.
The homing heart may joy or weep.
Yours is the wonder that is born
Of holding close all those who call
Your roof their own. Confide to boughs
About your eaves in spring or fall,
In June or now that life endows
A house with Christmas laughter
For now and ever after.

Photograph by Jessie Walker

Christmas is not a time or a season but a state of mind. To cherish peace and goodwill, to be plenteous in mercy, is to have the real spirit of Christmas. If we think on these things, there will be born in us a Savior and over us will shine a star sending its gleam of hope to the world.

CALVIN COOLIDGE

Beneath the Tree
Author Unknown

The crystal star was gleaming bright
From the topmost branch on Christmas night.
I sat alone, and icicles twirled
And twinkled at me from their tinsel world.
Beneath the tree, where gifts had lain,
The cross of the wooden base was plain
Through the cotton snow, and I was stirred
By a thought so true that I almost heard.
Beneath the beauty, the glitter and gloss,
No Christmas wholly conceals the Cross,
For there is a form that each must own,
Geometry of flesh and bone.
And Bethlehem's star can never die;
The heart's own cross will hold it high.

Photograph by Jessie Walker

The Wonder of Christmas

Elisabeth Weaver Winstead

In manger bed
    on fragrant hay,
The precious
    Baby Jesus lay;
Gentle Mary
    proud vigil kept;
The Holy Infant
    smiling slept.

Soft lambs and sheep
    beside Him stayed,
Warm shields from chilling,
    cold winds made.
Wise Men and shepherds
    traveled afar,
Guided by rays of
    gold-gleaming star.

Heralding angels
    chorused in flight
The gladness of
    that glorious night.
Rich gifts of praise were
    given to greet
The sacred Christ Child,
    precious and sweet.

A brilliant, bright halo
    encircled above
The cradled dear Baby,
    God's gift of love.
The hopes for joy
    and peace were born,
Our wondrous gift, that
    first Christmas morn.

Photograph by Dianne Dietrich/
Dietrich Leis Stock Photography

Reveries

Deborah A. Bennett

Hushed stood heaven's gentle angels,
Round the moonlight-frosted hills.
Hushed, the shepherds keeping watch
O'er flocks abiding in the fields.

Hushed, the stars in the pilgrim sky
Above celestial climes traversed.
Hushed, the Wise Men's greeting came
To mark the Savior's birth.

Hushed, with myrrh and incense sweet,
Their treasures they opened to Him.
Hushed, they heard the tidings of joy
That filled the stable dim.

All hushed as the Babe in the manger lay,
So soft in the nestling peace.
Hushed, as the streets of Bethlehem
Beneath the white wind's reveries.

And when they were come into the house, they saw the young child with Mary his mother, and fell down, and worshipped him: and when they had opened their treasures, they presented unto him gifts; gold, and frankincense, and myrrh.

— Matthew 2:11

DEVOTIONS FROM THE HEART

Pamela Kennedy

CHRISTMAS GIVING

I rushed in after a frantic day of Christmas shopping. After a brief look through the mail, I tossed it onto the end table, accidentally knocking over the Magi. (Ever since our daughter learned in first grade that the wise men didn't show up until a year or so after Christ's birth, she has forbidden us to put them anywhere near the crèche!) As I set the three kings upright again, I examined them more carefully. Each one held his gift: a little chest of gold, a vial of frankincense, a jar of myrrh. I reconsidered my recent frenzy of gift shopping. Was there something I could learn from these three little figurines?

First of all, their gifts were given with love. They had trekked a long way to find the newborn King, and,

Photograph by Jessie Walker

when they finally stood before Him, they fell down and worshiped.

Second, they brought gifts that cost them something, not an inexpensive trinket or bauble picked up at a strip mall along the caravan route.

Third, their gifts demonstrated an understanding of the recipient. Yes, He was just a young child, but they knew He was also a mighty king. They brought gold that spoke of royalty, frankincense that represented deity, and myrrh that may have presaged His suffering and death. These valuable gifts may have even made it possible for Joseph and Mary to finance their escape to and return from Egypt. If so, the gifts were also very practical. Was there a lesson here for me?

So often it seemed my primary goal was to check the box next to each name on my gift list, indicating that I was finished with one more recipient and could move on to the next. The

---

Dear Lord, may the gifts I give this Christmas be a reflection of the love You show me every day.

---

joy of giving, the love was maybe less than it could be.

I tried to remember times when I was really excited to give a particular person a gift. I thought of the year early in our marriage when I created handmade butcher aprons for everyone. We had little money, but I carefully chose the fabric and appliquéd different items indicative of the person's interests on the front of each apron. My husband's had a hamburger, complete with a ruffle of green lettuce peeking out from under the bun, and my father-in-law's had a black stew pot with red rickrack steam rising from it. They were not costly, except in time, but

they communicated that I knew something about the recipient and cared about him.

Another year I put together notebooks with old photos and original poems about our parents at different stages in their lives. My own children were recently reading through the one I had given my mother, asking her how she and their grandfather had met. The gift is still being enjoyed, over thirty years later.

I recalled the special gift my own daughter had given me just a year earlier. On a very slim, college-student budget, she had secretly taken a photo of my mother and me from the back, walking arm in arm across some sand dunes. The picture, in a simple frame, brought tears to my eyes when I opened it. What a treasure!

Maybe I have let Christmas shopping become just another holiday chore when I should be looking at gifts as an expression of love and caring, to be given from the heart—a reflection of God's gift to us over two thousand years ago. Maybe I could take a lesson from the Magi and offer gifts this year that demonstrated my love, a sacrifice of time, and my understanding.

Photograph by W. Pote/H. Armstrong Roberts

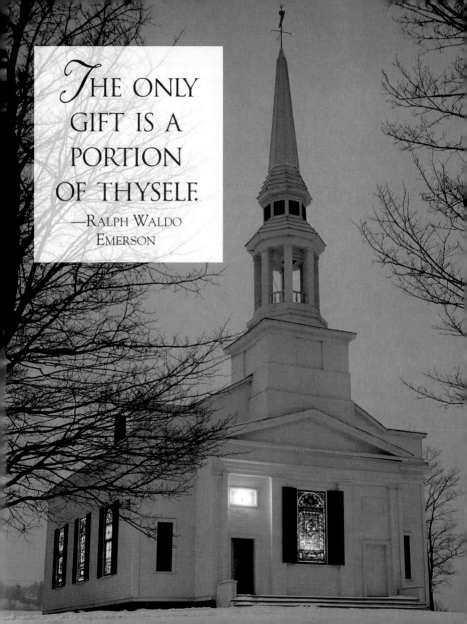

THE ONLY
GIFT IS A
PORTION
OF THYSELF.
—Ralph Waldo
Emerson

Christmas Grace

Miriam Snow Priebe

Dear Lord, on this,
    Your day of birth,
Our tree is bright
    with shining balls,
Our house rings out
    with cries of mirth,
Grandchildren play
    in the halls.
Throughout our home
    soft lights are gleaming;
Our table with
    rich food is spread;
And friends have come,
    with faces beaming,
To share with us
    in breaking bread.

You came, dear Lord,
    to humble stall;
Rough shepherds were
    Your guests that day.
You shared the warmth
    of donkey small
As You lay swaddled
    in the hay.
A heavenly star
    bright light was bringing,
And love shone from
    Your mother's face;
And angel choirs
    on high were singing
That You had come
    to save our race.

Dear Lord, on this
    Your day of birth,
We thank You for
    the food we share;
We thank You for
    these gifts on earth;
We thank You for
    the clothes we wear,
For warmth, and home,
    and love of friends.
We thank You for
    the life You bring,
Eternal life
    that never ends.
We praise You, Savior,
    Christ our King!

Photograph by Darryl R. Beers

Joseph's Dream

MATTHEW 1:20–24

But while he thought on these things, behold, the angel of the Lord appeared unto him in a dream, saying, Joseph, thou son of David, fear not to take unto thee Mary thy wife: for that which is conceived in her is of the Holy Ghost.

And she shall bring forth a son, and thou shalt call his name JESUS: for he shall save his people from their sins.

Now all this was done, that it might be fulfilled which was spoken of the Lord by the prophet, saying,

Behold, a virgin shall be with child, and shall bring forth a son, and they shall call his name Emmanuel, which being interpreted is, God with us.

Then Joseph being raised from sleep did as the angel of the Lord had bidden him, and took unto him his wife.

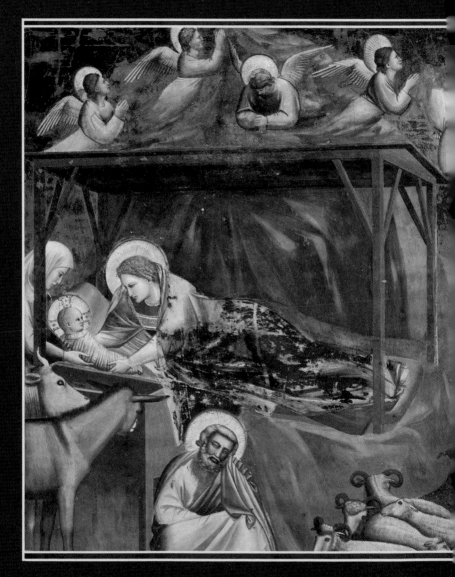

The Nativity

LUKE 2:1–7

*A*nd it came to pass in those days, that there went out a decree from Caesar Augustus, that all the world should be taxed. (And this taxing was first made when Cyrenius was governor of Syria.) And all went to be taxed, every one into his own city.

And Joseph also went up from Galilee, out of the city of Nazareth, into Judaea, unto the city of David, which is called Bethlehem; (because he was of the house and lineage of David:) To be taxed with Mary his espoused wife, being great with child.

And so it was, that, while they were there, the days were accomplished that she should be delivered. And she brought forth her firstborn son, and wrapped him in swaddling clothes, and laid him in a manger; because there was no room for them in the inn.

The Adoration of the Magi

MATTHEW 2:1–2, 7–11

*N*ow when Jesus was born in Bethlehem of Judaea in the days of Herod the king, behold, there came wise men from the east to Jerusalem, Saying, Where is he that is born King of the Jews? for we have seen his star in the east, and are come to worship him. Then Herod . . . inquired of them diligently what time the star appeared. And he sent them to Bethlehem, and said, Go and search diligently for the young child; and when ye have found him, bring me word again, that I may come and worship him also.

When they had heard the king, they departed; and, lo, the star, which they saw in the east, went before them, till it came and stood over where the young child was. When they saw the star, they rejoiced with exceeding great joy. And when they were come into the house, they saw the young child with Mary his mother, and fell down, and worshipped him: and when they had opened their treasures, they presented unto him gifts; gold, and frankincense, and myrrh.

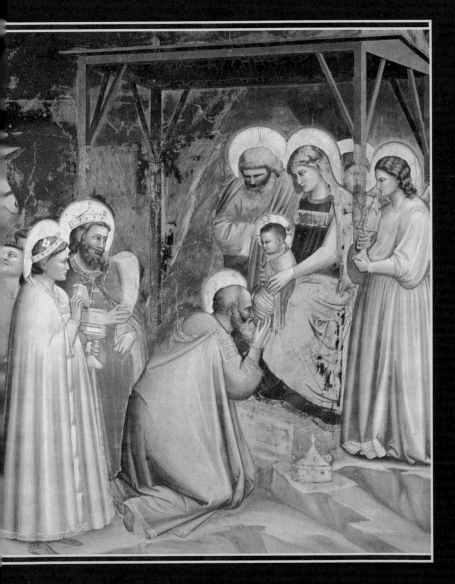

Presentation at the Temple

LUKE 2: 25–32

And, behold, there was a man in Jerusalem, whose name was Simeon; and the same man was just and devout, waiting for the consolation of Israel: and the Holy Ghost was upon him. And it was revealed unto him by the Holy Ghost, that he should not see death, before he had seen the Lord's Christ.

And he came by the Spirit into the temple: and when the parents brought in the child Jesus, to do for him after the custom of the law, Then took he him up in his arms, and blessed God, and said, Lord, now lettest thou thy servant depart in peace, according to thy word: For mine eyes have seen thy salvation, Which thou hast prepared before the face of all people; A light to lighten the Gentiles, and the glory of thy people Israel.

Flight into Egypt

MATTHEW 2:13–15, 19–21

And when they were departed, behold, the angel of the Lord appeareth to Joseph in a dream, saying, Arise, and take the young child and his mother, and flee into Egypt, and be thou there until I bring thee word: for Herod will seek the young child to destroy him.

When he arose, he took the young child and his mother by night, and departed into Egypt: And was there until the death of Herod: that it might be fulfilled which was spoken of the Lord by the prophet, saying, Out of Egypt have I called my son.

But when Herod was dead, behold, an angel of the Lord appeareth in a dream to Joseph in Egypt, Saying, Arise, and take the young child and his mother, and go into the land of Israel: for they are dead which sought the young child's life. And he arose, and took the young child and his mother, and came into the land of Israel.

Image provided by Scala/ Art Resource, New York

Christmas Reflection

Sarah C. Merrell

I hope my heart has heard the song
The shepherd heard that night.
I hope my heart has found the star
The Wise Men kept in sight.
Then maybe it will find its way
To the quiet manger too,
So the heart can kneel in worship,
Bringing gifts sincere and true.
My heart can bring no wealth of gold,
Nor perfumes rich and sweet;
But let it bring humility
And lay it at His feet.
It may bring loyalty and truth,
With love wrapped all around;
Then, having looked upon the Child,
Rejoice with gladsome sound.
For shepherds went upon their way,
Rejoicing loud and clear.
They spread good tidings so
That my heart, too, might hear.

Thou Whose Birth

A. C. Swinburne

Thou whose birth on earth
Angels sang to men
While the stars made mirth,
Savior, at Thy birth
This day born again;

As this night was bright
With Thy cradle-ray,
Very light of light,
Turn the wild world's night
To Thy perfect day.

Bid our peace increase,
Thou that madest morn;
Bid oppressions cease;
Bid the night be peace;
Bid the day be born.

Photograph by Darryl R. Beers.
Inset: Photograph by Gay Bumgarner.

Always Christmas

Kay Hoffman

There'll always be a Christmas
    Wherever our path may lead
As long as hearts reach out
    To help someone in need.

As long as little children kneel
    Beside their bed to pray,
"God bless the Baby Jesus,
    And help me be good each day."

There'll always be a Christmas
    With hope and peace again,
As long as there is caring
    And goodwill toward all men.

As long as there is faith and love
    To keep hearts warm and kind,
No matter where our path may lead,
    There'll be a Christmastime.

Christmas Bells

Mamie Ozburn Odum

The bells peal forth on Christmas Day,
Pleading the world to kneel and pray.
Each stroke comes sweet
The world to greet
With peace, sweet peace, on Christmas Day.

Christmas has come throughout the land
And brings the Christ-child to every man.
The story old, yet new,
A story old, but true,
Of peace, sweet peace, on Christmas Day.

The chimes peal out along the way
To bless the land both night and day,
A chant so sweet,
All hearts to greet
With peace, sweet peace, on Christmas Day.

Silently I pray, I know the need,
"Give us peace on earth," I plead.
"Remove the wrong,
Fill hearts with song
And peace, sweet peace, on Christmas Day."

The bells ring out with great elation
And reach the heart of every nation,
The right will grow,
Wrong fail, we know,
With peace, sweet peace, on Christmas Day.

Photograph by William H. Johnson

Christmas Chimes
Kate Strauss Shibley

Ring bells! Joy impart!
Every eager, hungry heart
Yearns to catch that angel song;
Ages echo it along.
It halts the throng
With listening ear,
Inspiration new each year.
Sing it. Live it, once again:
"Peace on earth, goodwill
    to men."

The Message
of Christmas Bells
Mabel Clare Thomas

Once more the bells of Christmas
Are ringing sweet and clear;
Once more our hearts are lifted up
And filled with hope and cheer,
For friendship knows no barriers
Of distance, time, or space,
And loving thoughts can wing
    their way
To any clime or place.

Each year the message of the bells,
Over mountain, plain, or sea,
Reminds us love is born anew,
Steadfast, tender, strong, and true,
Wherever we may be.

Photograph by Larry LeFever/
Grant Heilman

Who can be insensible to the outpourings of good feeling and the honest interchange of affectionate attachment which abound at this season of the year? A Christmas family-party! We know nothing in nature more delightful! There seems a magic in the very name of Christmas. —CHARLES DICKENS

An Old-Fashioned Christmas

Elisabeth Weaver Winstead

Let's have an old-fashioned Christmas;
What a day of delight it will be,
Hanging wreaths of spruce and cedar,
Bringing home the fresh, green tree.

Candlelight shines by each window,
Sprigs of holly on mantel and door,
Sweet aroma of gingerbread cookies,
Pies and puddings baked by the score.

Bright sleds skim frozen hilltops,
Velvet snowflakes in radiance beam,
Ice skaters glide like quicksilver
In the moonlight's golden gleam.

Make it an old-fashioned Christmas!
May each waiting heart feel the glow
That grows with the ringing of sleigh bells,
Drifting over the soft-silvered snow.

Photograph by Jessie Walker

COUNTRY CHRONICLE

Lansing Christman

WINTER BIRTHDAY THOUGHTS

This December marks my ninety-fifth birthday. In the winters of my past, I have learned that a bright beacon of hope is always there—winter sunshine. That beam of sunlight paves a protected path through this occasionally forbidding season and makes it easier for me to accommodate the ice and snow.

In winter evenings, other things ease me through the long hours. In the soothing quiet of the still, crisp air, the gleaming stars and glowing moon pierce the shadowy, snow-covered hillsides and create their own severe beauty. They remind me that the riotous colors of other seasons are not the only treasures of nature.

Inside, I enjoy the long, slow evenings by the fire reading my favorite books and reacquainting myself with old friends. The elderly calico curls up in one soft circle of pleasure beside my feet; stretched comfortably on the fireplace rug is the newest resident, the orange tabby who adopted this place last summer.

Perhaps a symphony or an opera will bring the exquisite joys of imagination to my evening hours. Songs of honor and love, courage and tragedy take me out of the confines of this cozy room.

I may also recall the winters of my childhood, when we sledded down nearby hills or skated on the farm pond. The laughter and the voices of brothers and sisters and cousins and friends still echo in my thoughts and make me smile.

Yes, with a few days of sunshine in the weeks ahead I will be content. The gentle touch of the sun's warmth will reach down from the bright blue skies, carry tomorrow's promise, and lessen the power of the storms that are yet to come. The days will begin to lengthen and bring with them a gratifying assurance of the cyclical motion of life itself. I know, after ninety-five years, that there is always a spring to come.

Photograph by Jessie Walker

December's Visitor

Eileen Spinelli

Christmas
comes calling
with pageants and wings,
with ribbons and holly
and popcorn on strings,
with boxes of tinsel,
with chestnuts and pies.
Christmas comes calling
with joy in her eyes.

Christmas
comes calling
with carols and bells,
with sparkling trees
and gingerbread smells,
with snowflakes and starlight
through cities and farms.
Chrismas comes calling
with peace in her arms.

Image provided by Fine Art Photographic Library, Ltd., London/Private Collection

Christmas Message

Luella Bender Carr

Beside the doorway a wreath is hung
Of cedar and cones with a tinsel bow,
And a cluster of miniature
    bells is swung
To tinkle a welcome. Now the snow,
Silently falling, tips with white
Each spray of cedar or tasseled pine,
And covers the doorstep
    snug and tight
With a snowy coverlet,
    smooth and fine.
Through the window,
    lamplight gleams
Warm and golden; its fingers seek
To reach beyond the pane. It seems
The night is articulate,
    waiting to speak.
Quietly I stand until,
All around in the hush, I hear
That age-old message of
    "Peace, goodwill"
Breathed into my listening ear.

Photograph by Dennis Frates

When we hear old, beloved carols
And crystal stars wink from the tree,
We read each card and old friends smile
From the corners of our memory.
—HELEN DARBY BERNING

Christmas Cards

Louise Dale Nelson

When the holidays are over,
And I have some time to spare,
I gather all the Christmas cards
And find an easy chair.
I pull up closer to the fire,
Take time to reminisce,
I read again each line and verse,
Lest something I might miss.

I try to pick the prettiest,
But I can't decide.
The ones I think on longest
Contain messages inside.
There between the pages
Is a special bit of news
About the crops or weather,
Or when the baby's due.

"I can't explain the way I feel,"
Says a friend as pure as gold.
But the simple words, "We love you,"
Make our blessings manifold.
The postman living here receives
A special one of beauty,
"Thanks for all the little things,"
Beyond his call of duty.

Oh, yes! The ones with pictures
We cherish most of all;
It's amazing how the children
Have grown to be so tall.
We sign cards with our heartstrings
And send them out to share
Our love and hopes for "Peace on Earth"
To people everywhere.

Photograph by Jessie Walker

THROUGH MY WINDOW

Pamela Kennedy

RUINING CHRISTMAS?

Whenever we try to add something new to our Christmas celebration or delete something old from it, we run into the objections of our daughter who complains, "But that will ruin Christmas!" She has the notion that only by keeping things exactly the same, year after year, can we annually recapture the joy and excitement of this, her favorite holiday. While I appreciate the way she cherishes family rituals, I think she has a bit to learn about the real value of traditions. Last year our Christmas tree became an excellent lesson.

A child of the Pacific Northwest, I never doubted that a freshly cut Douglas fir was the key to Christmas cheer. I remember the intoxicating scent of evergreen filling the corners of our home on the day my father set up the tree. Each morning, I would bury my face in the pungent boughs and breathe in the very essence of the Christmas season. In the evenings I would lie on my back with my head under the tree and gaze up through its branches, pretending I was in a forest filled with holiday grandeur. I was, in short, a true believer in the importance of a live tree.

Even after I married and the Navy conspired to have us spend Christmases in places like San Diego and Honolulu, where bushy Douglas firs were costly and difficult to find, my husband knew better than to suggest we get something else. That is, until the year we moved to Wisconsin. With three young children in a two-story wood frame house, we realized a dry Christmas tree could be a dangerous fire hazard. Very reluctantly, I agreed to purchase an artificial tree. But it had to look real, I determined, and we would get a wreath made of fir and pine boughs for the evergreen scent. My husband and I searched until we found an artificial tree that met our standards; then, with a bit of sadness and resignation, I decorated it. To my surprise Christmas was an especially joyous

time that year, filled with happy children, beautiful music, and a tree looking, if not smelling, like it had just been plucked from its forest home. A new tradition had begun and, although I can't remember why any longer, we named our little tree Bartholomew.

I would lie on my back with my head under the tree and gaze up through its branches, pretending I was in a forest filled with holiday grandeur.

For twenty years, Bartholomew Tree stood as faithful guardian over our holiday festivities. Last year it became evident that his needles were sparse, his wire branches bent, and he had taken on a definite droop. It was time to replace the tree.

Happily, we discovered that since our purchase of Bartholomew, the artificial tree industry had made great advances. We found a gorgeous, realistic-looking tree that was not only taller than our old one, but wider and thicker as well. And, as an added bonus, it had all the lights already placed on the branches! Once we had our new tree in place and decorated, we were delighted with the results. But we were sure our daughter, who was away at college, would fear the imminent ruin of Christmas. And that is when my husband came up with a delightful plan. He disposed of old Bartholomew, except for the eighteen-

> *The day our daughter arrived for Christmas break, we held our breath.*

inch uppermost section. This he mounted on a block of wood. We decorated it with miniature birds and tiny strings of frosted crystal beads and set it next to the crèche. There it stood guardian over the manger scene we had used ever since our first Christmas as newlyweds. Our intention was to use this little version of our old tree until our daughter had her own home, and then give it to her to begin her own Christmas traditions with a bit of the tree she had enjoyed from babyhood.

The day our daughter arrived for Christmas break, we held our breath as she rushed into the house eager to place her special ornaments on the tree. She stopped in front of the new tree, looked at it critically for a few moments, and then turned with a perplexed frown.

"You got a new tree!" she said, a trace of disappointment in her voice.

"Do you like it?" I asked.

She studied it for a few moments, touched the boughs, and traced her finger along the curves of red garland draped around the tree. "It's prettier, and bigger, but I guess it's just not the same. You know, our tradition."

"Not to worry," her father said, beaming. "Check this out!" He pointed proudly at the smaller version of Bartholomew standing guard over the Holy Family. "Now you can start your own tradition!"

"Oh, Dad," she laughed, throwing her arms around her father's neck. "You know me too well! I love it!"

I think I saw the gleam of a tear in her eyes as she kissed her father and realized that traditions are not so much rooted in things, but in the love that gives them meaning. And as long as that love remains, changing our traditions will never ruin Christmas.